50 TIPS ON DEALING WITH THE MEDIA

Make your interviews work for you

Guy Clapperton

Clapperton Media Associates

Introduction

Do you run a business or are you involved in public relations?

If your answer is "yes" to either of those things then you may well want to talk to the press to publicise your endeavours or your those of your client. So you attract a journalist's attention and go and see them or do a phone interview (even now they're not mad keen on video conferencing) and...it all seems to go a bit wrong. Sometimes the journalist is plain hostile and sometimes they control the interview completely. You've done a great job – for the journalist. You've done nothing for your business or your client.

I've been one of those journalists for three decades, starting in January 1989. I know many of the tricks and I understand why people would use them – many interviewees are trained to throw as much nonsense at us as they can, to prevent us getting to anything other than a bit of bland marketing. So we end up spiking the interviews.

This is why I became a media trainer in 2002. I believe passionately that people should have a fair chance to put their case and their view in front of the media, and to equip themselves with the skills and insider knowledge to make sure their message is heard. I don't help people lie and I don't help them cover up.

As part of this, I've been running a blog of media tips for many years. This "book" (I put it in inverted commas because other than a few trims and clarifications I have written nothing new) is a compilation of 50 of those entries. There will be some commonality of themes but I was pleasantly surprised to find there was very little overt repetition (no doubt readers will find some) and although I've dipped as far back as 2015, most of the advice is still current.

It's a book of blog entries and reads like it (you'll note that the keyword "media training" appears fairly close to the front of most of the entries, for SEO purposes); I recommend dipping into it rather than reading all the way through.

I hope readers will find the contents useful. Anyone wanting the "live" version (i.e. me media training them) is welcome to get in touch.

Guy Clapperton

March 2019

Guy@Clapperton.co.uk

Does your face do odd things in front of a camera?

I had a lively week last week with three media training sessions (in London, Cambridge, London) and a speech in Glasgow. The week offered a lot of learning for me as well as the people I was coaching. And this week's lesson was: what on earth happens to people when you stick a camera in front of them?

I handled one of the media training sessions with my friend Paul. a documentary maker who brings seriously professional kit with him every time. Lighting, big camera, he's got the lot as you'd expect from a professional. The delegate and his PR and marketing people greeted us and were perfectly friendly, Paul set up and we started the first interview.

Nobody is saying plastic bonhomie is a good idea on camera but the delegate's smile suddenly vanished, he frowned with that "this is how I look when I'm sucking a lemon" face some people get. I appreciated he was concentrating. It didn't actually look terrible on camera but it somehow wasn't him. He was a much more welcoming and open person than any viewer would ever have guessed.

In another media training session when I was flying solo but had my digital SLR with a mini-tripod on the desk, a guy who'd been equally welcoming and positively effusive about his company when I arrived didn't actually clam up but the smile vanished, he was suddenly very serious about his business (and I get that business isn't hilarious all the time) and – sorry to say this – a bit dull. Another person took one look at the DSLR, screwed his face up and clammed up completely. This was a senior director who knew his stuff.

Cameras are there to help

The thing to remember is that a camera is not there to catch you out any more than the journalist is. Large amounts of people seem to think that's all we're interested in, but that's not the case. A camera, in the right hands (and my colleague Paul in particular is very reassuring to delegates and never fails to offer brilliant advice) is there to capture what actually happens and who you or your client actually are as a delegate.

So in the same way that you'd prepare for a job interview and be respectful of the process, of course you should prepare for a journalist or blogger's interview and have an idea that it might make a difference to your business.

But as the advice always runs to younger job applicants, the best thing you can do is to be yourself rather than to close up. Also as your seniority increases, remember that in a job interview you can afford to be a bit more critical and have input into what the post is going to do for you; it's the same with media interviews. The more experienced you are, the more we're coming to you to take advantage of that experience – we're using you to make our reports look good. It might not feel like it but that actually puts you in a pretty powerful position.

So don't be put off by a camera – use it as a tool to help you, to be yourself and to relax into the interview a bit. This may take a few goes to get right and of course I'm available to help with dummy sessions. You'll end up with a clip that plays to your strengths and we'll end up with a better report. That works better for both sides.

Do you know your audience's culture?

I'm typing this en route to a media training session in Cambridge and I had another yesterday in London - and in London the question of culture came up. The client had been in the US and spoken to the press, and his financier had told him afterwards that he was "really British".

Well, fair enough, that's where he was from. But this had affected his media performance. He'd been factual and welcoming in his manner, he'd felt, but that hadn't worked in America.

Culturally dour?

In America the culture - and this is a vast generalisation - has more of a 'can-do' environment than in the UK. We are traditionally shy about our achievements (some people would say this is actually the worst sort of false modesty that is in fact a colossal conceit but I'll leave that to other analysts). His natural slight reserve had served to make his companion think he wasn't really selling the company.

So we tried an exercise in which the camera operator and I asked him to lift his energy levels in the interview. He did so and although they might not have reached "American level" if we could call it that, he ended up performing much better and communicating his message really well for just about any audience.

There's a lesson in here. If you're going to be interviewed on video a lot of the advice around says you'll be in close-up so you should just treat it as a conversation. There's something in this but you'll also be talking to a larger than usual amount of people so it can be worth raising your energy levels a bit. It's not a performance or a public speech but it's not a private conversation either - so adjust your tone accordingly.

Do you rehearse your quotes?

My media training offering includes a lot of 'dummy' interview sessions. In other words I'm the dummy who sits and asks the questions while you (or your client if you're a PR person) answers. I send a recording of the interviews, on video, after the session (and then destroy my copy).

In related news I'm speaking at the Professional Speaking Association's East Midland group next Wednesday and as part of my preparation I'm going through the speech, out loud (it's based on my Near Futurist keynote (see Nearfuturist.co.uk) but tailored for the audience, as the live versions always are). The dog and the cats are completely baffled by my behaviour.

Why am I doing this? Because I'm delivering a presentation to my peers and I want it to be right, obviously. That's no biggie. The audience will be in tens but they may be helpful to me, or better still I may be able to help them somehow. So of course I'm rehearsing, memorising most of it (I don't like word perfect speeches as they just sound pre-packaged). You'd expect that.

Now ask yourself, if you ever do press interviews, interviews with bloggers, podcasters etc...do you rehearse your answers?

I'm rehearsing because I'll be in the room with tens of people. If you speak to me for my podcast then I'm actually quite excited to say you'll be heard by many more - it's now hitting thousands of downloads per month. If you go onto TV, even local TV, you can increase that figure; go into the national press and you're talking about hundreds of thousands, go onto national television to make your point and you're likely to be watched by millions.

I repeat, you took it as read that I should rehearse for tens of people - and you were right. And yet so many people go into the media with a rough idea of what they want to say but not much more. Whether businesspeople or politicians they can end up sounding uncertain and hesitant not because they don't know or believe their stuff but because they haven't practised or worse, they haven't prepared.

When you have a media interview coming up it's worth practising, trying to anticipate the trickier questions and having answers ready, and sounding confident and fluent even if not super-slick and artificial. It always makes a better impression in front of a person of influence, whether that's a journalist, podcaster, blogger or anyone else.

So what if you hesitate?

One of the things people ask in my media training sessions is how to avoid hesitating when they answer a question. I can see why. Earlier this week former Labour leader Ed Miliband was on the Today programme on BBC Radio 4 and the show's anchor, John Humphrys, asked him something. He paused and Humphrys said: "You're hesitating".

Here's the Tweet I put up afterwards:

John Humphrys just said to Ed Miliband "you hesitated" on asking him a question. No doubt he thought he had him on the ropes.

Actually that's the sound of someone thinking before they answer. I'd be happy with a bit more of this in politics.

— Guy Clapperton (@GuyClapperton

I don't intend to show off when I say that Tweet had 99 likes when I typed this blog - just to illustrate that a lot of people agreed. That may have peaked but it's quite a lot.

I encourage hesitation in my media training

One of my old contacts from my days on the trade press used to hesitate a heck of a lot. I'd call him at 3Com, where he was MD, we'd exchange pleasantries and I'd ask questions. There would then be silence.

Once I actually asked: are you still there? His reply was: "Yes, that's the sound I make when I'm thinking". (I do enjoy a good comeback, even when it plays against me - I once had an editor who explained to a colleague that I was "saving up to be a half-wit", which I thought was pretty good).

So now ask yourself: what sort of journalist would object to that pause? I'd asked someone a question that made them consider rather than trot out some sort of pre-prepared soundbite. That's surely a good thing for an interviewer, isn't it? Certainly the readers get a better deal if someone offers a thoughtful response.

In the case of the Today programme they're dealing with politicians who expect a tough time and who are prepared, prepared and prepared again before going in front of the microphones. It's probably fair to check and see whether a pause is actually a sign of something more significant. For most purposes, though, thinking before you speak is good practice rather than something to avoid.

Even if the journalist thinks you're showing weakness, the likes on my Tweet suggest the audience - and those are the people who actually matter - will disagree.

Do you overthink?

Media training last week threw out an interesting point. How much overthinking do you (or if you're a PR professional, your clients) do in an interview? Are you turning it into too much of a performance? It's not something theatrical, it's a conversation, but some people treat it as something different.

I asked one guy a fairly straightforward question. "So, your device does basically one thing and this is it, is that correct?" He shut his eyes. He thought a bit. He pondered. It was a whole minute before he replied.

"Yes," he said. Later I asked him what was going on in his mind. "I thought you might take it as a forecast; I didn't want to paint myself into a corner where I said we were only ever going to do the one thing, I didn't want the quote catching up with me later," he said.

I'd been after a simple fact check. He thought there was a lot more going on.

Sometimes there is no agenda

Years previously I did a session in which I began by asking one of the people there: "Tell me about yourself and your organisation". She panicked. "What is this...why would he...can we stop the exercise?" Of course I stopped. I'm not there to distress people. She then asked why a journalist would want to ask about her, why I needed her to disclose anything personal.

She was stunned and felt a bit like kicking herself when I told her that a simple "I'm NAME/JOB TITLE of COMPANY and we do LINE OF BUSINESS". It's all I wanted. It was effectively the journalist clearing his throat, just making introductions.

The point is that people often feel the journalist (or podcaster, or blogger, or whoever) must be up to some sort of trick. They have an agenda. And we do - it's to write interesting stories that engage and inform our readers. I'm not going to be stupid enough to say there's never an agenda - but very frequently a "hello" is just a greeting. Overthinking will make you self-conscious - and that's when the interview starts to get a bit stilted.

A word about story telling

A journalist likes to tell a story. Facts and figures are essential but they may not be our main focus; we need to engage our readers. Not everybody realises this so we get a lot of data-based story pitches.

Imagine a picture of two horses grazing in a field. There is a bus stop behind them so they must be near a road. We'll come back to their story in a second.

Years ago, before we all had WiFi, I media trained a client that specialised in data compression. They could do an awful lot and explained to me just how compressed their data could be, gigabytes down to megabytes, saving transfer time when the files moved around.

I'll be honest, I could barely stay awake. They admitted this was true of most journalists they spoke to but not their customers. One buyer in particular had to maintain submarines and relied on an ungainly 40-volume-long technical manual. So the maintenance operative would have to get into an uncomfortable and potentially unsafe position, examine components, come out, check the technical manual and go back in, sometimes more than once.

My client had compressed all forty volumes onto a single phone. So the engineer had to make only one trip, with all the information now portable. They told me this over coffee and it was a revelation when I explained to them that they'd just brought the whole thing to life. Never mind the bits and bites, I had a mental image of this operative risking his or her safety and comfort repeatedly, and the difference their technology made. The stats on how this happened were important as a support and would make sales happen but the story I could tell my readers was about people. Anyone could understand it.

Now, about those horses.

The horses' story

In one way I've told you everything about the horses - grazing, two of them, bus stop, field. That's the solid factual information.

If I tell you the description is of a picture on holiday a few weeks ago in an unseasonably sunny October it starts to sound livelier. If I tell you the horses actually lived in the fields that backed onto the Sussex holiday cottage we'd hired and that we like it so much it was our tenth visit, and that we celebrated my wife's birthday there this year, the story has a lot more colour to it. I could tell you about my daughter seeing those horses for the first time when she was about seven years old...excuse me, something in my eye...

I could tell another story. I could fill in the technical stuff and say I was experimenting (OK, playing) with my phone's camera, the Huawei P10 Pro, to see what it would do with a distance shot - the horses were about half a mile away. I could tell you I cropped the shot to get the horses about two thirds of the way down the picture, which makes for a more interesting composition than dead centre, and I could add my disappointment in finding that there was a bus stop in the background, which I couldn't see with my naked eye.

The facts about the quantity of horses and what they're doing don't change but the amount of colour I can add to them by putting them in context is massive. You don't have to find it thrilling and you might well react with "how come you think the horses' story is about you?" but you can, I hope, see the point. The bare facts, data and statistics can indeed be a thing in their own right, or they can support a story a journalist or other influencer is going to find easier to tell his or her readers. Why not see if your or your clients' facts can be adapted to do the same?

Use humour carefully

A lot of my media training sessions include a lot of joking around from the delegates. I enjoy this - it lifts the tone of what could otherwise be quite a heavy session and if journalists are the butt of the gags a lot of the time, fair enough. It's actually pretty productive.

That's as long as it doesn't spill into an actual interview too much. Humour can work to break the ice with a journalist as well but you can't always take it for granted. They may not be on the same wavelength as you. If they're not of the same nationality and culture, humour can be best checked at the door.

Say what you mean

I had coffee with a colleague recently. She had been quoted as saying she didn't really know how to do her job but had lucked into it and often resorted to guesswork. On this occasion she hadn't actually said any such thing and a glance at her output would confirm to anyone that the idea was absurd. The blog was taken down.

It occurred to me, though, that when someone asked me about how I balanced the articles in the magazine I edit, between academics and analysts, I told them I aimed for an even mix of articles I understood and articles I didn't. To me that was an obviously flippant comment and luckily the other guy understood it as that.

However, if he'd taken me literally, the idea that I didn't understand what I was editing could have spread.

Other cultures

The issue becomes even more acute when you're talking to people from other cultures. There's a great book called "Watching the English" by Kate Fox, in which she notes that if you ask an English person what they do for a living and they say "This and that, not a lot really" then a British listener will understand there's more to it; a German listener will assume the person is between jobs and not ask further.

This isn't what happened to my misquoted colleague but it's the sort of minefield you can open up if you're not a little cautious when you're using humour in an interview situation. It's not natural to be completely straight-faced most of the time for most of us, but here are three basic tips to keep you out of trouble:

1. Try to restrict humour to the intros, particularly if you're nervous - give a serious question a serious answer.

2. Check the background (or get your PR people to tell you) of the interviewer - they may not share humorous or indeed cultural references you might want to make.

3. Read the room - if your quips are falling on stony ground, try to restrict their use.

Not everybody is prone to cracking gags every five minutes but I know a number of people who are, whether in media training sessions or elsewhere. Be judicious with your use of humour rather than use it as a scattergun defence against your nerves and you should be fine.

Why doesn't the journalist understand your story?

In media training sessions I'm asked why people get misquoted. The fact is that in interviews someone can make a mistake. Sometimes it's the journalist and sometimes not, but here's a thought: how carefully do you explain what's going on?

When I started in this business I was very young (no, I was) and I didn't know a lot. I was working on the tech press but only because I'd applied everywhere that might have me for nine months solidly, three applications a week, and finally found a billet in the IT space. I knew nothing about it - I'd been in admin and the deal was that they'd teach me journalism if I tidied the filing. Which I completely failed to do but that's another story.

So I'd be in front of an interviewee and they'd say "do you know about distributed computing?" Or their company background or whatever else I needed to know to write the story.

Nowadays I'd say "no". If it's something I might be expected to know, I could even say "can I have it in your own words, for the readers". Aged 23 there was no way I was admitting I didn't know something. So I'd confirm I knew all about it - and after the interview, as you can imagine, I made a fair few mistakes.

The fact that I'm still in the business (I still write as well as offering media training) tells you that none of them were particularly serious. But what if they had been? The chances are, as I was a trainee, my editor would have made allowances. The interviewee might not be so lucky if his or her boss wasn't in a forgiving mood.

The unfortunate fact is, no matter whose fault it is and how easy it is to amend afterwards online, a misconception can cause quite a problem even in the short term. And unless you know the journalist understands your business, it's in your interests to spell everything out.

So if you're in technology, make sure they've done more than use an iPhone - or be prepared to go jargon-free and explain the basics in simple terms. If you're in music production don't assume they understand the ins and outs of a mixing desk just because it's natural to you. If you're in food production always check that they understand the implications of a hygiene certificate rather than make assumptions.

And that's before you've taken it as read that they appreciate the importance of a particular move or promotion within the company. They may not. Actually it might not even be that important to the outside world - and if not, it's up to you to sell us the idea of writing about it. But try to make sure we understand all of the main pillars on which the issue sits.

A journalist or blogger will feel foolish if they get it wrong. They may even find their position jeopardised, but that's not your problem. It's in your interests as well as theirs to help them get it right, first time, so your message is clear immediately.

A correction is a good and honourable thing, but damage can happen before the amendment is put in place. Always try to make as sure as you can that the initial version is the correct one.

Who's on the phone?

An excellent afternoon media training in Reading yesterday threw up an excellent tip about using the phone. Most interviews are on the phone these days so there are some practical points to bear in mind.

First, try not to be on the phone by yourself. If your words are mangled or misquoted you might want corroboration to demonstrate that you weren't quoted correctly. Equally, in some instances you might benefit from someone else being on the call to point out that although you didn't mean the words as they appear, they're what you actually said. A sanity check either way is useful.

However, I always tell people not to assume the journalist has cleared the line before you ask your colleague or PR representative for feedback. End the call and call back separately. I once interviewed an inexperienced (I assume) business owner for the Guardian. She was professional, helpful, a real pleasure. And just as I was about to terminate my side of the call, I heard her say "I was sh*t, wasn't I..." - I nearly reassured her, realising just in time that the worst thing I could possibly do would be to let her know I'd heard that.

We established the point but then yesterday's PR person said: always assume the same at the beginning of a call. He was right. Journalists might well hang around hoping to catch a bit of chatter after a call, but if we dial in and hear you going through a list of things not to mention - the MD's walked, half the sales force has just joined the competition, whatever - we might well not announce ourselves in too much of a hurry.

The delegates then added that journalists might find the "call in early, hang up late" trick easy if they are on a large conference call. One of the delegates had been on a call with 31 other people only the previous week.

I can't make this clear enough. Unless it's a staged and largely scripted call (say, financial results, or a major new product release or something), it is going to be very unwieldy to have too many people on the call. More than two or three, particularly if they have similar accents, and we're going to start attributing quotes to the wrong person (you know your voices well but honestly, we don't).

As far as is logistically possible, the ideal call is you, the journalist and an independent PR person who can verify what was actually said or not, and maybe cough loudly when you're about to give away a trade secret.

As the marketers say, Keep It Simple, Stupid!

How often should you mention your brand?

I was media training a client a few years ago. The internal PR person was in the room as well. The delegate did well in her first dummy interview - until the internal PR person said they weren't mentioning the brand often enough.

In fact, in a 10 minute interview, the delegate had slipped the brand in about three times. I thought that was about right; it was there but unobtrusive. The internal PR person insisted it should be put in about seven times.

I rarely disagree with the internal PR people whilst on the premises but on this occasion I had to. That many brand mentions, I said, and the delegate's quotes would end up on the cutting room floor. "Well, we'll just have to agree to disagree, and my instructions are to mention the brand more," said the internal PR person.

The company did a few interviews but didn't get quoted much. It was as if someone had told them this would happen, and why, in advance.

Mention the brand, but...

You do need to mention the brand if you're in a media setting. Another media training client, in tech security, had been onto breakfast TV. He assumed his job was to promote the brand by being intelligent and thoughtful. He would be introduced as "from XX software" and the credit on the screen would give his job title and company, so he didn't mention them, just aimed to offer the viewer the very best advice so they'd come to the company afterwards.

His interview was excellent. People learned stuff. Unfortunately, one thing they didn't learn was where the guy worked; he was introduced as "Guy's Client, technical expert" (not his real name, weirdly enough) and the caption on the screen said the same thing. He had no idea until he'd finished that he'd got up at 5am and done literally nothing for his company.

There's a balance in there somewhere. I stand by my original thought that a mention about once every three minutes (and yes this takes planning and being aware of where you are in the interview) is about right. Ending up on the cutting room floor or being too shy to mention who you work for won't achieve anything for you.

Is your spokesperson available?

You or (if you're in public relations) your client can gain a lot from good media training. One thing that will stop it working, however, is the client's unavailability.

It happened to me only recently. I was looking for contributions to a magazine I edit. A PR person got in touch with a pitch, and contrary to the impressions some journalists give out, it was superb. Well targeted, understood the brief and wasn't at all phased by the fact that I wanted more than 300 words. When, they asked, did I need it?

I gave them a date a few weeks from now. They came back to say their client was on holiday. Oh. This happens when people are issuing press releases as well. I have a good idea of whose fault it is and above all else whose fault it isn't.

PR people need to push back

The PR community is absolutely not at fault here. Client has announcement, client insists announcement is made, announcement happens, they follow all the rules a media training session might advise on targeting, structuring of the press release, whatever else. The release has a "for further information please contact..." note on the end so the journalist emails or picks up the phone.

And the client is away. He or she is unavailable precisely when the journalist or blogger or other influencer needs to speak to them.

This is where the PR community needs to push back.

Media training can help, but...

A session with a media trainer or journalist can help a lot to set client expectations but in these instances the PR people really need to be on the case. They need to tell the client they have to be available if they want to secure coverage. This may mean delaying a release by a fortnight until they're back from holiday. It may mean broadening the amount of spokespeople who can speak to the press. It is never going to mean the journalist holding onto the story until the person is back; if we perceive that the story is old, we won't touch it.

Most people in business work to deadlines but there is often some flexibility. They may not understand that it isn't the same for a news site, that we won't hold off publishing something until we know perfectly well it's a fortnight old. It's up to the PR consultant to take the word "consultant" seriously and to advise the client. We get that stuff happens and sometimes someone really is called to a meeting, there genuinely are family crises that need their attention or whatever. For the most part, though, we need people to be available when they're drawn to our attention.

Otherwise we're unlikely to take you seriously next time.

Storytelling 2: be careful

Media training sessions almost always make one thing clear: a business needs to engage people rather than just push facts and figures out there, so telling a story is a good idea.

Well, yes. On the other hand, here's a story about one of my interviews.

An executive was coming over from America and his PR people had persuaded me I should interview him. Fine, I said. We met up in London and just to warm the meeting up I asked him whether he knew the city particularly well.

"Sure," he said. "I was a student here. I lived in a flat in Covent Garden for a year."

Impolite though it was, I couldn't help myself. I asked. How on earth does a student afford a flat in Covent Garden for a year? Granted the guy was a little older than me so would have been staying there in the late seventies/early eighties but it still wasn't cheap, even with a student grant.

"That was the funny thing, we got it rent free," he said. "The owner was a singer and just needed someone to look after his flat while he was on a world tour. You know Dave Stewart?"

Not everyone is going to be familiar with 1970s/1980s pop, so I'll fill in a blank if you need it: Dave Stewart was half of a band called the

Eurythmics, Annie Lennox being the other half. They were huge and among my favourites.

And here's the problem: this guy was there to tell me about his software company, of which I'm even a customer (and no I'm not going to embarrass them by saying who it was). However, from the moment he'd told me about living rent free in Covent Garden for a year in a rock star's flat, I wasn't remotely interested in anything else he had to say.

Tell stories by all means but make them salient. And try to make sure your central message is as interesting if not moreso than the story you're telling.

A sort of tenuous postscript to the Dave Stewart story happened more recently. I was considering joining the Hospital Club in London, waited in reception and was shown around by a very pleasant membership executive. On one of the walls there was a poster for a Dave Stewart gig.

"He's one of the owners here, isn't he? I like him a lot," I said.

"Ah, he does a few gigs here. You're not a massive fan, though?" She replied.

"Oh, I think I am."

"OK," she said. "Just maybe not quite enough of a fan to notice you were just sitting next to him in reception for ten minutes?"

Oh.

The question isn't personal

Sometimes a question is all about context and you can read it all wrong. In a media training session last week I asked just such a question in an exercise and the delegate felt "got at". So what can go wrong?

The answer can be more to do with what's in your head at the outset than what's in the journalist or other influencer's question.

What did I ask?

The delegate in question (and my delegates are confidential so I won't name him) had founded a business 15 years previously, employing eight people at start-up. The organisation was now listed and employed some 400-500 people.

My question was: "What learning and skills have you had to pick up on the way, so that the person who founded the thing with a handful of people is still the right leader 15 years later?"

In my mind there wasn't a problem. He'd have learned loads, built teams, explored markets. There was a lot to be learned from his answer. He, on the other hand, felt a bit attacked. It was as if I'd asked him: "Come on mate, it's just you, who are you trying to kid?"

His reaction had to be more to do with him than to me. He was expecting a bit of hostility and filled in the blanks so that he found it.

The moral of the story is pretty simple. Journalists asking questions are almost invariably going to be filling in the blanks and finding out what makes you tick. They aren't going to be trying to catch you out and we may even hope to learn something ourselves. There isn't necessarily an agenda to cut you down to size - and after 15 years in business, building an organisation to 40-50 times its original scale, I don't think I'd have been able to if I'd tried.

Don't insult the journalist!

Press interviews are a great way to get your message to a large number of people. Unfortunately sometimes they go wrong as happened to Elon Musk this week, who managed to tell journalists that their questions were "boneheaded".

Here's the big secret: in interviews, journalists sometimes as stupid questions. Maybe they don't know your field terribly well, maybe as in this case you want to talk technology but it's a specific call to discuss financial results, as this one was. Maybe they're just boneheaded.

Here's the other big secret: not everybody likes journalists. It may be unfair to write off swathes of people when all they share in common is a job but genuinely, some people just don't like us. Nonetheless it can still be a good idea to work with us.

I had this once. I was interviewing someone from an old IT company, Sun Microsystems. I don't remember what I asked him but I do remember this senior executive from the States telling me I'd asked a boring question. I smiled sweetly and suggested he livened it up with a decent answer. He looked as though a hundred volts had gone through him - I think he thought he'd shut it down.

So if that's you or your client, what do you do?

At the risk of sounding old-fashioned, the first move is to go back to basically being polite. You don't have to call a journalist "sir" or "madam", and we do get that some people think we're basically parasites. But if one of our number is standing in front of you, don't tell us we're boring or boneheaded. You might have clients whose intellect you don't rate. That doesn't mean you'd stand there and tell them so.

Well, we could have thousands of potential clients among our readers. So if you give us a bad impression we can pass it on, really easily.

If you find that difficult, then a good second move is to remember you're on the company's time rather than your own. OK, you don't like journalists. Dislike us in your own time - you're being paid to talk to us so talk to us civilly.

Third, try to see it from our point of view. We're there to write a story and we need some quotes to go into it. So our questions might be unduly basic, they may focus on our readers' needs (which may well be financial) or our perceptions of them when you want to talk about something like cool technology. We have no less of a job to do than you do, and compromising is always going to be useful.

A postscript is that Musk's share price fell 7% after his financial results came out. Granted there were solid business issues as well but I do wonder whether the drop would have been quite so severe if he hadn't been so reluctant to talk reasonably about his financials.

Ask your media trainer a sensible question

I do a lot of media training and very often people start with an email from a PR agency. On many occasions the first thing they want to know is how much I charge.

Let that sink in for a moment. They ask about the cost before finding out whether I'm the right person to help. They are actually in danger of buying an off-the-shelf offering that may or may not help their client. If it does, fine. If it doesn't, what's gone wrong?

Why do you want media training?

A better option is often to start with a conversation. Make contact by email by all means but as soon as we can, let's get on the phone. My media training page on my website and this blog will give you an idea of where I may be coming from but they're a taster rather than the whole thing.

During our initial conversation I'm going to try to find out why you're calling. I don't always finish by offering media training. If you're looking for extra sales and want a direct result from any coaching I may offer, then a sales push rather than any input from me is probably a better idea. I know PR companies who have achieved huge coverage for clients and then had complaints because sales didn't follow immediately. That's not how media coverage works every time. If I can't deliver on your objectives I'd rather not have the business.

There are often other reasons. You might, very straightforwardly, have seen a competitor doing well on a TV interview, in a blog or in the press. I can help you or your client get to the same level of polish. You might be anticipating a crisis or a difficult press interview, or you might be nervous of appearing in front of a camera. I can coach you for those things. Your client might have seen the competition making themselves look silly by producing badly-written articles, guest blog posts and other assets. I can help with writing skills or even help with the writing itself (so I'd be advising against media training and recommending writer coaching or some other service you needed).

You might be asking for some sort of help in a specialist niche of which I know nothing, in which case I'd be urging you towards one of my colleagues who'd know more about it and could do a better job. If I'm not going to be the right person to help I'd much rather say so up front and pair you up with the people you need.

The best outcomes for a client always come from asking the right questions and knowing what you're after. So if you get in touch about media training, don't be surprised if I ask why you need me first. I like to tailor my approach, and getting to the reasons you're asking will help me to make sure I answer your actual needs.

Expect the unexpected

Last week I went onto the Jeremy Vine show on BBC Radio2. The subject was the practicalities of switching your mobile phone from Apple to Android. The last caller said she had an issue because her friends with Android phones kept sending her texts in which her name was autocorrected to the word "Vagina".

The team thought she was probably a real caller with an issue. Personally I have my doubts; the late, great Peter Cook apparently used to call phone-ins with a made-up voice just for the hell of it. This could well have been one of those.

Nonetheless, I was left with this going out live and had to decide what to do. I doubt that many readers will have to cope with exactly that situation (I hope!) but let's say someone throws you a curve ball - how do you cope?

Don't panic

The first thing to do is to stay calm. I made a small joke about being thrown - that was easier because there was more than one of us behind the microphone. A journalist who's throwing you a trick or provocative question is after a reaction. It's better not to reward them.

Then take the question on its own terms. If it's something you can't comment upon for reasons of client or employee confidentiality, say so, politely. If it's something you just don't want to comment on, bridge away, politely and gently. If you need time to think, the phrase "let me think about that for a second" will buy you time (people often ask me what tricks are available when they need time; the straight answer is, none, just tell someone you're going to take time).

Personally I gave a straight answer and then caught myself refusing to believe this was a real call. Nobody, repeat nobody, addresses one of their friends as "vagina" repeatedly and doesn't notice, no matter what their autocorrect does. If you're giving interviews for your business you're unlikely to get the spoof call but rushing into a poorly thought through answer is rarely going to deliver a good result.

Interviews: you're allowed to say stuff

I media trained someone last week whose default position in interviews was to give as little away as possible. She was worried the journalist or blogger would get something she didn't want them to have. Her initial objective was to say not very much and shut up.

Fine, but what does that view do for your business? I've seen the cautious approach in interviews go spectacularly wrong a few times, and I've seen the other extreme too.

Interviews in which you don't say a thing

In my last staff job I once interviewed a guy who'd sold his company. I asked how many of the staff were keeping their jobs. He was very stilted in his answer, which was along the lines of: "There will be a number of changes as a result of the new ownership of the business."

OK. I asked whether he would be staying on and got exactly the same response. "There will be a number of changes as a result of the new ownership of the business."

Apparently once I'd left the PR people gave him quite a rocket. They suggested, quite rightly, that he'd sounded as though he had something to hide. Since he didn't, this was quite galling for them. The truth was that he'd spent a decade building a business, created a load of jobs, most of which were continuing, and it was time for him to have a break and enjoy the rewards. Instead, I ended up with a picture of a rather shifty individual who gave the impression he thought he was up to no good.

All because he'd decided not to answer a straightforward question, for no good reason.

Interviews in which you say too much

The close cousin of shutting up too early is of course blabbing about everything. I interviewed a company - at their invitation - that did invoice factoring. This works to ease cash flow; you issue an invoice, send it to them instead of your client, they pay you and invoice the client. If the client pays late they do the chasing.

I gave them my business card, which said "reporter". I asked who they worked with and they named several blue chip companies.

They were then horrified when I mentioned that I intended to name the companies in print. "But that's confidential, you can't!", they said. I didn't, but I had every right to. They had expected - hopelessly naively - that I would travel all the way to their office and write what they instructed from their brochure (note: this is not what journalists do, it's what happens when you pay a copywriter).

On another occasion I was interviewing a guy about an early attempt at an Internet device, this one aimed at elderly people. This was September; he told me the version in February would be better because it didn't have sharp edges and the Internet connection would be free. I wrote this and then had a complaint that I'd as good as told people not to buy the existing version.

Neither of the two interviewees had any sensible reason to tell me those things. On the other hand, the first interviewee gave me the impression something was up.

It's therefore worth making a couple of lists before every media engagement. First the "they're bound to ask" list, effectively an FAQ. That should be easy to ascertain, probably with the help of a PR person or company. Second the "I hope they don't ask" questions and what you're going to do with them.

Third, the neutral stuff - just find out what you're allowed to speak about and what you're not. People sometimes get tied up about whether they can name any clients, even when their employer names them on its website so the information is already public.

Get a briefing. Find out what you can and can't say and have a strategy to avoid the questions you can't answer, and remember "I'm afraid that's company confidential, can I help you with something else?" is a perfectly reasonable answer even if the journalist or blogger doesn't find it personally helpful.

But please, don't assume that dodging even the simplest of questions is clever. If you really don't want to talk to journalists, don't do it - agreeing to talk and then clamming up is just going to look odd.

Yes of course I know the answer without asking, but…

I'm interviewing you, I ask you a question. You think: surely he knows the answer to that? And yes I might. So why am I asking?

There are actually a number of reasons a journalist might ask you a question to which we already know the answer. Here are two scenarios.

First we go back a few years, but the principle is up to date. I was working at a trade newspaper for computer dealers, called MicroScope, in the early nineties. At that point personal computing was just kicking off; the Internet wasn't widespread but it existed and there were very few retailers selling IT.

Oh, and everybody with a 'build your own computer' book was going to topple IBM as the market leader. It was no use arguing, they just were. So we'd get calls into the office, very frequently, from someone saying they were starting up a manufacturer and would be charging less, people were stupid for paying over the odds for a name.

We would start with the stupid questions. Were they going to use an operating system, we asked. Would they be including a motherboard (at the time this was the bit into which you inserted the processor, memory and all sorts of other bits).

If the caller sounded unsure, we knew we were talking to a time waster. (The caveat here is that even if they knew a bit more, they might still be a time waster but it was a useful enough initial screening).

A question for an established player

You can see that sanity checking is a reasonable use of the apparently stupid question. It works particularly well for the new company and to assess how realistic or knowledgeable they are even once they've mastered the basics of their product. I once media trained someone who believed their service could target "everybody". But who are you aiming it at, I asked. "Everybody!" they replied, not suspecting that if a company the size of Tesco didn't market to everybody, the five of them were never going to do it.

Another use applies to the more established player. To use an example from the previous paragraph, I'd never seriously expect a director at Tesco not to understand the retail market. I might, though, ask her whether the company proposes to continue operating from retail premises rather than going online. I know perfectly well it's not going to shut all its stores overnight, so why am I asking the question?

The answer is in the implied rules of journalism. Yes, I know the answer, but I need it in your words. The rules - of news reporting and feature writing at least, opinion columns are another thing - state that my interviewee's words are worth a lot more than mine. The reader, listener or viewer wants me to explain or summarise but I am not the story. The interviewee is the expert and I am not. So yes, I will ask you a question to which I know the answer. It doesn't mean

I'm stupid, and the occasional incredulous response "Surely you know that?" tells me more about your briefing or your understanding of the interview process than anything else.

Should you give a journalist a gift?

I come to your press launch and get the story with a load of other journalists. You give us an Echo Dot, Echo Spot, a television, a rucksack, whatever. Should we be influenced by that when writing the story?

The answer is of course we shouldn't, simple as that. And yet all of those items have been given to me or offered for attending an event. Someone on Facebook was asking what they should give journalists at a press conference and it's set a lot of people thinking about ethics. So here's my take:

1. Think very carefully about whether you need to have a press conference at all. If it's a good story rather than a put-up job, journalists and indeed bloggers should be inclined to write about it anyway. An email or phone briefing might get you the coverage you want.

2. If you're going to attract journalists to attend, it may seem reasonable to offer them something in return. I've attended launches of smartphones where you get to take the phone away with you. In order to write about it intelligently you need to use it for a while. So if it's something strictly relevant, as in that case, I don't see a problem.

3. Likewise an event I intended to attend (but was prevented) last year on artificial intelligence, at which the giveaway was an Amazon Echo Dot. They're not expensive and it was in the interests of the company involved to get journalists or bloggers using some sort of AI regularly.

4. Sometimes it's a matter of branding. I've had more laptop bags than I'd normally know what to do with and the family has been very pleased, but I get the need to have your brand out there. I have unused memory sticks coming out of my ears and that's before you get started on the corporate branded biro.

5. Moving into 'more of a present than a help' I've had two instances of small Android tablets with the press kit on them - which have of course ended up formatted and given to family members. In cases where everyone attending a conference is given the same thing and the journalists get the same package, fair play - it probably costs you more to put different packages together than to give everyone an identical bag.

6. Pre financial crash, and particularly in the 1990s, journalists were offered all sorts of stuff. I attended one launch of a network router and was asked for my address so they could send a portable TV by way of thanks for attending. It didn't make the router any more

interesting. On the other hand, more recently, I was shown around a Portuguese site of a contact centre and given the corporate rucksack (of course), which contained a book on Portugal and some of those custard tarts they make over there. They weren't strictly relevant but I could quite understand that as a foreign visitor they wanted me to have something local to their country, of which they were fiercely proud.

There are some hard and fast rules in the gifts-to-journalists business. First, if it feels as though you're bribing us, that's probably what's happening. Relevant samples of your product are different (try publicising food and drink without allowing journalists and bloggers to find out what it tastes like and you won't get very far). Second, there are publications that will decline gifts, limit themselves to gifts of a certain value and in some cases actively avoid events at which gifts are distributed. If you're doing something international you should be even more careful; I did a panel in Turkey a few years ago and the Muslim journalists were actively offended by companies they perceived to be offering inducements to attend something.

The safest bet, to my mind, is to offer an excellent story we can't get elsewhere. If it involves a product we need to try, fair enough; otherwise if you want to offer us some sort of memento, maybe don't tell us in advance so it's not an inducement to attend - and do what they do in the public sector, make it either very low value or perishable so we won't just stick it into the office raffle.

That's the theory, anyway. In the real world, competition for journalists' and bloggers' attention is fierce and the PR community will try a great deal to get us to turn up to things. Sometimes this involves gifts and inducements. We're as human as anyone and if someone has thought to get us something nice, we're likely to be pleased. Just don't, whatever you do, think you're buying positive coverage. An ethical journalist or blogger will be very careful not to be influenced by any sort of material blandishment; if you're in PR and your client is talking about showering gifts on people offering coverage, make sure they're aware that the best of us will remain independent!

Beware your media comment, it will haunt you

Today of all days, be thankful you're not Toby Young. If you're unaware of the guy, he's just been appointed to the board of a higher education watchdog. It was not a universally popular move.

Part of this is due to his politics. He is a self-declared Conservative and the incumbent party of government always gets it in the neck. Also because he was allegedly viciously critical of state educated kids in a Spectator piece a few years back. He's added a final paragraph at some point which kind of digs him in further; if you have to explain something wasn't offensive, it probably was.

Essentially, you can't disown something once you've said it. A provocative journalist like Young will understand this.

So what if you made an unhelpful media comment?

The problem is that some of us who've been around in the 1960s and previously might have said all sorts of things, whether in the form of a media comment or otherwise, over a lengthy-ish period of time. So, what do we do about them?

The first thing is to check them at the time. If someone has genuinely quoted you out of context, make the point, politely. However, make sure it really is out of context; wishing you hadn't said something does not make it out of context at all.

For example, when the foreign secretary [*Boris Johnson at the time of writing*] said his comments about whether a British aid worker was on holiday or training journalists were "taken out of context" when doing a bit of wriggling before Christmas, it was wrong - the whole interview is available and the context is clear. "Out of context" does happen but not that often. I've done it myself but only for humorous effect; many years ago Lord Alan Sugar had an issue in which people were complaining that his Amstrad computers were overheating. He denied this and came out with the quote: "We don't need fans, it's all rubbish, but if people want them, we'll put them in." Then he bought the football team Tottenham Hotspur, so the magazine on which I was working at the time resurrected the quote - deliberately and in a humorous section, so nobody thought he was actually talking about Spurs fans. It was out of context but on that occasion harmless fun.

So, is something out of context or not?

Second, allow yourself to change your mind. Just say so. Nobody should mind as long as you don't do it all the time about things you said only last week.

Third, allow yourself a screw-up or two. Last year, Prue Leith accidentally gave away the winner of the Great British Bake-Off on Twitter (she was overseas, got her timings mixed up and thought the episode had been broadcast). Her response when questioned was "I f***ed up". It was unfortunate but she didn't wriggle, she faced it head on.

By now we're all aware of how quotes can follow us around so my final thought is to suggest drafting something and then leaving it for a while. Does that thing really need to be said, even on Twitter? What's your objective, and would it be better served by a polite rephrase?

That last point might have cost Donald Trump his presidency if he'd heeded it during his campaign, so let's not pretend every rule applies everywhere. Mostly, though, it pays to be aware that everything you say in public may be repeated and scrutinised just when you don't want it to be. Be prepared, have a response and remember, they were your words so you must have meant them at the time!

Read the paper

Getting into the media can do a lot for your business. One of the better ways can be to place an article. You write it, so although it will be adjusted for style (so that if they write % rather than per cent it will be consistent throughout the publication) you're in control, nothing's going to be taken out of context.

So why do so many people not bother doing the basic research?

Size matters

A couple of weeks ago I had a pitch from someone for a magazine I edit. It seemed a pretty good pitch and the subject was more or less in the area we write about. I had a quick call with the PR person who said she'd get some bullet points back to me so we could sharpen it up.

So far, 10/10 for process and approach.

An email then arrives.

Her client had gone ahead and written the article ahead of the briefing. BIG MISTAKE. Even if you're going to write an article in advance, no editor is going to want to think your piece is that unfocused. We want to publish articles that target our readers exactly, so it's in your advantage to give us the impression that you've taken our requirements into consideration.

I open the article. The word count tells me everything. It's 650 words long.

The publication I edit works in 500-word blocks because a page takes roughly 500 words (it's still on paper). Yes, an editor can always cut, but we don't publish single-page articles either.

I made the point by email to the PR executive. I haven't heard back - given that the guy had written the article in advance she's probably hawking it around elsewhere hoping someone will take it. She has little choice.

Time to push back

The difficulty really came up when the client decided to write something without taking the target into account. This is where the PR consultancy needs to take the word 'consultancy' seriously. The value you can offer is in pointing out that some things just won't work, and writing a neutral article hoping to catch a niche readership is one of them.

Of course the client might then decide that risking a tailored article, useless to anyone other than the target title, with no guarantee of publication, is not a good use of their time. At least you have them thinking about what **is** good use of their time!

You know what you mean but will I?

Media training twice last week was a treat. The best sessions always throw out something new and this was no exception.

I asked one of the delegates what he did. He said he was the head of SE for his business. That's interesting, I said. What areas in the South East specifically?

He and his colleagues roared with laughter. They thought I was joking. SE meant sales engineering, and he was in charge of Europe plus bits of Africa. I'd been about to ask him about his prospects in East Grinstead.

The point is, I wasn't joking. When I hear SE I think "South East" as a reflex.

Media Training for comprehension

This is why I always encourage people to take any jargon they may have in their interviews out and shoot it. SE isn't the only example. A couple of years ago I was in a proper interview, all grown up. There was a PR person, the director at their client and someone they introduced as one of their "SMEs".

OK, I thought, small to medium business, this is good, he'll be here because he's used the service. So I started by asking what he did for a living. He looked puzzled, shrugged and said he was one of the company's SMEs. Yes, I said, but what do you actually do?

After a while it emerged that SME in this case meant "subject matter expert", he worked for the PR company as an expert witness might work for a court.

There are probably plenty more of these and the difficulty is that when you're at work, you probably use them without a thought. They're common parlance. If you're talking to a journalist, however, be very clear and spell out any acronyms, or better still don't use them.

The exception is when you're writing something and want to make a point. I was once writing a white paper for a client and they asked for a glossary. I put as the heading: "Why TLAs cause confusion", and the sub-editor insisted I spelled out TLAs (three letter acronyms) out. It made sense but it sort of filleted the headline.

Are you being recorded?

Many journalists use voice recorders rather than take notes nowadays. So what are your rights as an interviewee if you find you've been recorded without your knowledge?

Personally I take a pragmatic view. Although in the UK, where I'm based, the Regulation of Investigatory Powers Act (RIPA) has all sorts of provisions for not telling someone you're recording them, it's not really about journalism.

When I'm media training I'm a little cautious about the law and that's because of the increased importance of untrained people doing the reporting. Only yesterday I was coaching a guy who's involved in an area that attracts a lot of bloggers.

Unlike some older journalists I'm not anti-blogger at all. Many are excellent and have more influence than journalists because they know what they're talking about, are the recipient of the service they're discussing, and so forth.

The thing is, they're not trained. They have log-in details for something like WordPress, perhaps like the one I'm using now; they have enthusiasm, they have knowledge, but it can't be taken for granted that they know anything about RIPA or its predecessors, or any libel laws or other issues journalists take for granted.

This can lead to the odd difficulty. A few years ago a family member was involved in a voluntary organisation, as chair. She decided she wanted her time back so after four years she stepped down. I was surprised when, a year later and two chairpeople later, a local blogger suggested she'd been deposed in favour of the current incumbent overnight. I pointed out his error and his response was that the organisation hadn't told him of the changes so it was therefore their fault. That would have been an interesting one to defend in court.

The problem was that the blogger had no real conception of it being his responsibility, not that of an outside body, to ensure that his words were true and accurate.

So we get to recording. Many bloggers and a number of self-taught journalists will be unaware of their obligations as regards recording an interview. Personally I tell people in advance and offer the interviewee a copy of the recording afterwards so that they can check their quotes for accuracy in the event of a dispute.

If I'm interviewing you, though, you need to assume I'm keeping some sort of record. It may be a written note or it may be a literal recording, but if I'm not keeping a record I'm not doing my job.

A side note is that journalists' notes, like recordings, will stand up as evidence in the event of a court dispute. So it was bizarre when once I asked a psychologist if I could record our interview and he said he was happy with my taking notes but a recording might enable his clients to identify themselves and he had to be careful about this. About a decade later I'm still trying to work out why he thought this would be any more of a risk with an audible record than with a written one, as long as it was accurate. It makes no sense at all.

The main point, though, is that you have rights of course, and if you feel strongly I'm not going to suggest you don't act upon them. But if a journalist or blogger isn't going to keep some sort of record in order to quote or represent your view accurately, why would you be talking to them?

When you're right, shut up

Some of you might recognise the quote in the headline up there. It's from a poem by Ogden Nash and the complete quote is "when you're wrong, admit it; when you're right, shut up". But what has this to do with interviews?

The fact is, it's useful advice for media interviews as well as life in general (it's probably saved many marriages). Your competitor may well be going down the pan. People might actually be stupid to spend money on a named brand rather than your offering. But is telling them so through the media going to do any good?

Trumped

You'll probably be familiar with the president of the USA's Twitter habit. Earlier this week he used the social network to respond to criticisms about how he handled a conversation with a war widow - a Gold Star widow in American jargon. She said he made her cry by saying her husband knew what he was getting into and not remembering his name. Here is his Twitter response:

I had a very respectful conversation with the widow of Sgt. La David Johnson, and spoke his name from beginning, without hesitation!

— Donald J. Trump (@realDonaldTrump

Now, I don't know Trump and I wasn't there. I'm no fan but in fairness, some of the comments on his Tweet indicate that there is a recording and transcript around (I do ask myself why) and that Trump may have a point.

From which I conclude that a distressed widow might not have been thinking completely rationally. This isn't a surprise.

Let's assume, then, that Trump is factually correct on this occasion. I still contend that the president of the USA, the most powerful man in the world, going onto Twitter and implicitly suggesting that a gold star widow is being dishonest, is unwise. He has overlooked the weight his office carries, he's forgotten the emotional state she is likely to be in. His wording is actually quite moderate but it doesn't matter - in the context of his other Tweets, this is seen as lashing out.

I've come across other examples. There was an elderly woman in America who gave interviews about how the tobacco companies, by marketing their product as harmless in previous decades, had effectively killed her. The lawyers cottoned on to the fact that she's worked with asbestos so it wasn't clear-cut. The PR people's counsel was that it didn't matter whether the tobacco people were right or wrong; massive cigarette corporations going after an elderly, dying woman in the courts was never going to look good.

So let's take an example that might occur in a more everyday situation. A disgruntled and fired employee is spreading malicious gossip about your company.

You can dismiss these as from an unreliable source. You have proof of his or her dishonesty and can furnish the press with it. But should you? Is this going to look any better than the most powerful president in the world criticising a widow for inaccurate recollections at probably the most difficult time of her life?

OK, it's not going to be **that** bad. But sometimes, even when you're right, shutting up can be the better part not only of valour, but of coming out not looking vindictive at the end.

Aim for a big finish

The best novelists know where they're going and plan their finishes first. So do the best interviewees in press interviews. Is it time you started?

I've been working with my friend Paul in our media training masterclass just lately, which consists of some fairly intensive interviews and feedback. One of Paul's best pieces of feedback is that people should aim for a strong conclusion.

This might seem less important if you're working with the written media. One of my worst habits in communication is that when I'm making a point I tend to tail off at the end rather than finishing well. That doesn't matter in conversation and in a written interview, nobody's going to transcribe the last "er..." which may be what you actually said. So it doesn't matter, right?

Be memorable in press interviews

The thing is, the journalist will have no choice but to go away and write finish the sentence for you. Of course there will be notes in press interviews, maybe even recordings, but essentially when we start writing the lead-in tends to consist of what stuck in our minds as important.

That last tailing-away "er..." isn't going to be it. However, if you go into an interview certain of the points you need to make and then make them, and summarise them at the end in an upbeat manner, we are more likely to use your own words.

This is never emphasised better than when Paul records something, plays it back to participants and they see the difference for themselves. They also pick up all sorts of other repetitions and habits they hadn't noticed before, and as an experienced cameraman Paul supplements my own media insights with all sorts of visual and audio tips.

There's no substitute for solid content of course, but presenting well visually is a skill worth mastering. And no, you don't have to be a supermodel to look fine on a screen.

Do journalists like facts and figures?

Media training a couple of weeks ago I was struck by one delegate's insistence on coming out with a statistic for everything. He was a businessperson, the readers were businesspeople, they'd welcome everything being backed up by a solid fact.

It's difficult to argue with that on the surface, but I'll have a go. The fact is that businesspeople might not like dry facts with everything but they need them. Let me put it this way: the business community deals with facts and figures all the time but only when it's pretty much being paid to do so.

The journalist's job, in the majority of cases, is to take up what happens after that.

Would you read dry facts over coffee?

Basically the dry business stuff is dispensed with, the coffee comes out and someone picks up the paper, the tablet, the phone, whatever they want to read on. At that point they're interested less in the raw data and more in the stories behind it.

This is why, for example, when I was writing extensively for the Guardian's small business section, they always asked me to get pictures of the people involved even when the story was about the difference the technology made. All of their research said that people buy from people and people want to read about people, so putting human beings on the cover was better than a screen grab or picture of a shiny new phone or something.

Technology has changed but that central truth hasn't. So if I'm interviewing you about a new widget you've invented and your stat says it enables a 10% time saving, why not tell me about what someone did when they'd saved that time? Or how they were able to grow the business steadily without employing someone they could ill afford, or something like that?

Show me a human face and tell a story whenever you can. By all means use the stats to support the story, but that's what they are - a support. My job is to relay stories; tell me a few and it could be to our mutual benefit.

Don't pitch me your story, pitch me a headline

I led two masterclasses on pitching yesterday, at a PR company I won't disclose because my clients are always confidential. One thing became apparent during the session: everyone wanted to pitch their client to me.

Which sounds perfectly logical. But it's not.

One of the delegates came out with something like this: "Hi, I'm calling with a photo-opportunity. My client is coming to the UK and will be making a speech to his/her employees, and you'd be welcome to come along with a photographer.

Her colleagues congratulated her on the pitch and her manner was indeed superb. The pitch, however, would most likely have died on its backside.

The pitch isn't about you, it isn't about me

The problem with the pitch above is twofold. First, it's all about the client. It doesn't have to be about me, whatever some journalists tell you, but it's absolutely got to be about my readers. Consider it again: there's a photo-opportunity (which sounds a bit manufactured anyway), there's a chief executive and there's a speech.

I know nothing about the content or whether it's going to be relevant to my readers at all at this stage.

The second problem is related to that first one: the delegate had actually pitched me the process, the mechanics of what his or her client was doing, and stopped there. You get limited time with a journalist on the phone. Why would you focus on the process rather than the content? (Come to think of it, why **do** so many people phone me and start "I'm just giving you a call"? I know that bit already...)

Start at the end

Here's the way I'd do it. Start from the final output you're looking for. Imagine you've prompted me to write an article. It's in the paper, on the web or wherever, and you're happy with the coverage and the headline.

Ask yourself: what does the story say? And what's the headline?

Now back in the real world, pick up the phone and pitch me that headline. Never mind the process, never mind that your client has done a survey of 3000 clients, never mind that your organisation is in the top ten widget suppliers to the small business market in the UK - that's background.

Lead in with the story. Tell me that your client has found that half the people who believe they understand IT security still have the default passwords on their phones. Tell me that your business has enabled someone to increase productivity by 30 per cent, meaning they've avoided making redundancies. Tell me why someone's life is better because of your client.

In fact, just tell me the story. If it's a good one I may well be interested.

Is your news timely or just new?

News, you might imagine, is something that is new. The word itself - although sometimes reported to be derived from the initials of the four compass points (I've never found any actual justification to that claim) - has a clue in the name, a patronising creep of a news editor once told me. (I'm not bitter).

Except when your audience isn't ready for it. A couple of decades ago, the Internet and email were brand new, or at least just coming into popular public use. I'd been freelance for a few years and was pitching to the Independent.

A story came in from the US, about how the .co.uk and .com addresses were going to run out by about 2001 (we now know this was not right, but we didn't at the time). I pitched it and then editor of the technology section thought it might be interesting.

I wrote the story and was surprised when something else appeared instead. The editor had spiked my story and put in something about how to set up your email address for the first time, something I'd assumed was already pretty elderly for the national papers.

If it's news to your audience it's news

The editor may have been right of course. In 1997 or whenever it was, home computing was just starting. The fact that web addresses may or may not have been in danger of running out may have been a

refinement too far for the readership at the time.
Many would be buying their first computer,
wondering what an ISP was and connecting to the rest
of the world for the first time.

If you're in PR or are pitching stories to the press
yourself, it's worth asking not just whether something
is new but whether it's newsworthy. This means it's
relevant to the readers and not something that may be
relevant in a few years. Certainly it shouldn't be
something that they just won't understand yet.

It's possible to risk patronising the readers as a result.
In 1997 I just don't know whether that editor was
talking down to his readers or whether the story I'd
pitched would have been way over their heads (why
he commissioned it in the first place is a question I
still can't answer). But always, always try to
understand your target outlet and address it rather
than address the things that might seem important to
you or your client.

Pre-interview nerves

Tomorrow I'll be presenting at the Professional Speaking Association's spring convention and nerves may be an issue. People often ask how I deal with them and the answer is that I don't, always. It's not even a big piece of presentation.

Whether you're about to be interviewed by the press or waiting to go on stage, nerves can be a problem. Here are five points to help you manage them:

- Embrace them. Nerves basically mean you want to give of your very best, make a good impression and deliver what the person or people in front of you want. You're not arrogant enough to take your ability to do so for granted. Good. Your nerves are a reminder that you respect the audience and want to give them something good.

- One theory a comedy mentor once relayed to me is that we go back to our instincts often. We're still cavemen underneath it all, so where there's a crowd, we expect to be facing the same way. At a press conference or anywhere there's an audience, the crowd faces us. Instinctively, at some level, we think they're going to kill us. They're honestly not. Recognising where your nerves come from is one way of combating them.

- A good way to overcome nerves is by preparing. First, make a list of the questions you're anticipating and make sure you have answers. Second, make a list of all the stuff you're hoping they won't ask - and have an answer for those too. If they don't come up, that's fine.

- As I've said elsewhere, remember the people asking the questions may not have a particular agenda other than finding stuff out. I once did a media training session in which I kicked off by asking one of the delegates: "Tell me about yourself and your organisation." She freaked out, asked to stop the interview, and asked why I wanted to know anything about her. In fact I was just warming up, a name and job title would have answered my question perfectly, but in *her* mind there was a dangerous agenda being set. Watch out for overthinking and assuming there's going to be this big agenda before you've even started.

- Don't give interviews or presentations for which you're unprepared. Now, "prepared" could mean a bit of deliberate prep for the interview backed by 25 years in your industry, but make sure you're the genuine expert in what you're speaking about. The people to whom you're speaking will then want to hear from you and no matter how hostile they may look (and a straight face from someone who's just paying attention can look *very* hostile if you're feeling tense), they're mostly on your side.

Will my readers be interested?

Targeting matters if you're trying to get a journalist or blogger's attention. Several times this week alone I've had pitches that start off "I've enjoyed your writing" and then continue with "your readers will be interested in my/my client's viewpoint/product..."

In principle this should be excellent. The sender has thought through who my readers are, which publication I write for and why the readers will want to hear from them. I should be excited.

Except that one of the pitches was for a toy (I have almost never written about toys, certainly not for five years or so). Another was for a restaurant launch (I am a technology and business journalist, you can argue that a restaurant is a business but it's tenuous).

One of the pitches that might actually have been in my area but was a bit vague prompted me to respond: where exactly were you pitching this? I do write for more than one outlet, after all.

Good targeting enables you to send a good reply

Dismally, I didn't get a response to that question. Literally nothing. This was a shame because I was prepared to listen and, once I knew a bit more about the story, consider where it might work best.

Presumably, bothering to send a response would have been too much effort. A second possibility is that the PR person involved took my query as a rebuff; I've had that before. I once told someone with a reasonable pitch that we needed a customer to talk to in order to make the story work, and he said "Yeah, I suppose you're right" and hung up - when I'd have used him in the Guardian quite happily if he'd gone and done the leg work.

A third possibility, and I fear the most likely, is that the pitch hadn't been targeted at all. The fact that it might have worked for me was a coincidence, and I was one of many journalists getting the same "This might work for your readers..." pitch, when the sender had no idea who the readers were.

Always, always find out about the readership you're approaching through a journalist or blogger. You'll be able to have a much more intelligent conversation afterwards if you have an idea of what you want to get out of it.

Watch out for keywords

I'm writing a small story for a new client at the moment. It's a fun piece. It's aimed at small retailers and it's specifically about sale events (and yes, I'm writing this in advance so it won't appear online until the piece is public).

The site is aimed at small independent resellers. There's generally better money in writing for the big guns, they have more finance; I do enjoy writing for and about people who are tiny independent businesses like mine. It's about sales - as in sale events, January sales, that sort of thing.

Some of the pitches have been very good. They took all of the above into account. Some are not.

Size can be important

One of them, for example, was from a major High Street store. Now, I have nothing against major High Street stores. But if someone is writing about and for smaller businesses, a pitch like "here's how Sainsbury's does it" is only so much use.

Another went: "The thing to do is to capture every customer's detail from every sale. Track them, send them the relevant offers and ensure you have a relationship."

All good advice in general but how does this relate specifically to the one-off sale event, I asked? Oh, came the reply, it doesn't. I thought you meant selling in general.

Which wouldn't have been so bad if they hadn't already been back to their client to source several paragraphs of good but completely irrelevant sense.

You only read one word, didn't you?

The problem in both cases, and yes I did ask, was that they'd just seen the word "sale" and sourced a load of verbiage that seemed vaguely relevant. They hadn't done anything about the detail, so they'd missed the fact that the client was irrelevant in one case and the subject was way off beam in the other.

I have some sympathy. PR is a pressured job. But as I've often said to my daughter when she's coming up to exams, taking the time to read the question first can literally save hours working on something that's literally never going to produce anything like a good result.

A journalist may not be a specialist

Journalists don't know as much as you think. At least not every time. People assume we're experts and that we know loads of stuff. We may have fewer resources than you imagine.

A friend of mine is a composer. He was on Facebook a while ago complaining that a noted contemporary composer had his name pronounced incorrectly on a small radio programme on the BBC. I pointed out that the announcer may have been stuck making his best guess, and my friend said "I imagine there's a team of researchers for them to consult".

Laugh, I nearly...

Journalists do their own research

Here's the big secret: Google has pretty much killed any advantage journalists had in terms of research about an interview into which they're going "cold". You can see the effect in a few stories that came up recently in the news.

You'll recall, perhaps dimly, that a while ago there was a huge fuss about Labour Party leader Jeremy Corbyn's tax return and whether he'd declared all of his income. He had not declared a full year as leader of the opposition.

Now, I'm also someone who submits a tax return, as a company director. So I'm well aware of the tax year running April to April and personal returns being due on 31 January, at least until the latest reforms kick in next year. People employed by other people don't have to concern themselves as much about those deadlines.

So it was perhaps no surprise that the many staff reporters writing up the stories didn't stop to think that if Corbyn submitted a tax return on 31 January it had to cover the year ended 6 April 2016. And since he wasn't leader of the opposition for the full 12 months before that, it would actually be factually wrong for him to declare a full year's income on leader's pay.

So many of the press didn't spot this. Likewise, they're not all specialists in how legislation works. Today's headlines (like the one in the Daily Mail: "Tory tax retreat after just 24 hours: Theresa May steps in to pause the £2billion Budget blow to the self-employed after a rebellion by furious Tory MPs") refer to a climbdown by the prime minister. But is it?

The original plan was to increase taxes on the self-employed from April 2018. Instead of debating it now while everyone is furious the PM is now going to have the debate in October, which will allow plenty of time for new rules to be enacted before April, indeed there will be another budget at around the same time.

Remind me: what's actually changed, other than the presentation?

So, why am I telling you this? The answer, quite straightforwardly, is that you can use it. Journalists may have limited resources. They may not all be specialists in the area in which you work (some will be, never be afraid to get a PR company to find out). We need to sound authoritative when we write, and that's where you can help.

Yes, you'll want to push your company's agenda. Yes, you'll want to use an interview to publicise your business. You can also use it to brief the journalist on stuff he or she needs to know.

When I started as a tech journalist I wrote a lot about printers (livin' the dream...). One contact was very helpful: not only did he tell me about his company's products, he took the trouble to explain exactly how the printer worked and how the contents of the toner drum ended up looking like words and pictures on paper.

Obviously, every time I needed extra comment on the printer market I'd go straight to him. He picked up a lot of extra coverage for his business.

There may be ways you can do the same. Is there something in your announcement that may not be obvious to a non-specialist? Is the publishing professional in front of you **really** a specialist in your field?

If he or she isn't, you could be in a position to pick up a hell of a lot of brownie points without even trying.

Make your quotes mean something

A meaningless quote is a no use to me - so why do PR companies insist on sending them? I can see the mechanics, but it really doesn't work.

Here's the theory. PR company notes that, say, the Queen is opening a new National Cyber Security Centre in the UK. Rather than wait for calls from journalists who may be covering it, PR is proactive and sources a quote or five from client on the subject, and sends them to the likely suspects - people who, like me, might be covering the event.

Most often, the journalist won't be covering the thing, but occasionally you strike paydirt. Today I was writing about it.

Only, there are some things I won't quote.

"Today's opening of the National Cyber Security Centre (NCSC) by the Queen demonstrates a new era as we continue our journey in the digital age"

OK I admit it, I've just quoted that here. But it didn't go anywhere my news story.

What are you really saying?

The subhead says it all, really. I had other quotes sent to me. One said the government couldn't handle everyone's cyber security needs by itself. Another said the issue wasn't government money but a skills shortage.

You see how these examples actually take the story on a little - not massively - but they do take it further than "this is a jolly good idea, then".

And that's what I need. If you can't deliver it, then you won't deliver for your client - nobody who wants to write anything readable is going to repeat a platitude if they can possibly help it.

It's worth the PR fraternity bearing in mind that the job involves consultancy rather than just parroting everything the client wants. It can be worth pushing back and telling them something's not going to work; the better clients will listen to expertise and hey, they might even come up with something better!

Five strategies for awkward questions from the press

A good press interview should serve your business well in terms of branding but it can go wrong. What do you do, in advance of the event and during it, to make sure things stay under control? Here are my top five tips:

1. Accept that it's not completely within your control. The journalist, blogger or other influencer doesn't work for you so a control-freak approach isn't going to help. Offer us the tools to build you a good piece of engagement and we might well respond, but we're not your marketing department.

2. Before the interview, make a list of questions you think we're likely to ask and prepare an answer. Make another list of questions you'd rather we didn't ask and prepare answers for those, too. Forewarned is forearmed and that sort of thing.

3. If you can't tell us something, say so. "That's company confidential", "We don't disclose that as a matter of policy" and other honest declarations are fine. We might not like them but if we don't work for you, it's equally true that you don't work for us. If you can't help, say so.

4. Be aware of what you can and can't answer, and above all be aware if something is in the public domain. I once asked a guy about his company profits. He said they were confidential. I pointed out that I could just go to Companies House. He replied - and I treasure this moment - that all Companies House would tell me was the figure he'd given them, his **actual** profit was much higher. I was very young at the time and didn't quote him on that. I've regretted it ever since.

5. If we're really pressing on something with which you're not comfortable, remember you're the expert in your business, not us. You can lead us into your comfort zone with phrases like "I think the important point is.." and "My customers are actually telling me..." - I can't argue with customers.

Those techniques ought to help with some of the trickier questions. Of course if you've been siphoning the company pension fund off and we've got wind of it and am writing a story about it, there probably isn't much you can do about it but we're probably the least of your worries!

PR professionals, time your pitching!

5 January and the poorly-timed pitching is in full swing. Even in an age of instant publication, journalists will have planned roughly what's in their schedule - outside the news - in advance.

Let's put it another way: there is no point, repeat no point, in asking me if I'd like a round-up of technology predictions from your client for the new year for the New Statesman, Professional Outsourcing or any of the other publications in which I am involved.

The reason is very simple. The beginning of the year was not a surprise. It's been in the calendar for some time. I was therefore able to plan for it and ask people for considered round-up tips, if I wanted them, in early December or even before that.

Pitching Christmas in July

Journalists have a tradition of "Christmas in July", by which we mean that the consumer goods companies wanting to publicise goods start to push them to is in the middle of the year. Many of them have special launch events at that time of year.

The tradition dates back to older publishing technologies, when in order to get into a monthly magazine's Christmas pages you really needed to get into the planning for July so that they would finish the relevant section of the issue for (probably) September, go to press in October and come out in November.

It is now easy to shorten the timescale of course, but "think ahead" is never a bad mantra in Christmas. Here are some mistakes I still see:

- People pitching 2016 round-ups - it's 2017 now, guys, I've checked

- People pitching 2017 forecasts as late as this morning. I want my readers to think I'm up to date, not trailing a few days behind everyone else!

- People pitching Easter/chocolate stories in the week running up to Easter Sunday. First, it's too late, second, I tend to write about business and technology rather than chocolate so have a think about where you're pitching.

- People linking their technology story to irrelevant items in the news. I appreciate that piggybacking a relevant story is probably a good idea, so "Startups are doing well in CES but my client has just got funding for her technical widget without leaving her sofa" is fine. The pitch I had roughly this time last year saying "David Bowie was a great original who always delivered. Software also has to deliver..." not so much.

A lot of it is common sense. Some of it is good taste. A handful of practitioners, however, don't seem to have thought about how their target publications are produced - or they're being measured by how much pitching they do and don't actually care.

Have an argument in public – we'll love it

One of the golden rules of media engagement is not to have an argument when the press is looking. It's too much fun for us to report. There have been good examples in the media very recently.

They come from the top, too. Our government has taken to falling out in public in the UK, and if the opposition weren't tearing itself to shreds at the same time more people would notice. Lately we've seen:

- Boris Johnson telling Saudi Arabia some home truths as he sees them - and being slapped down by Downing Street immediately;

- Former education secretary Nicky Morgan criticising Theresa May for spending money on expensive designer trousers, getting banned from Downing Street as a result and most recently getting criticised by a Tory grandee for trivialising the Brexit vote.

So, other than annoying the government - and believe me there are plenty of examples from the other side, just consider the attempts to unseat Jeremy Corbyn over the summer - what do these stories share in common? I'll tell you: they are the most brilliant fun to write about because we love to see the rich and powerful making fools of themselves and falling out.

But if you were to do something similar in business, how would it work out for you?

Market shares

When I first started working for the technology press there were two stories I wrote every month. They had similar topics and covered market shares from software companies. First, there was the periodic row between Microsoft and WordPerfect over who was ahead in the word processing market.

Each claimed leadership. Each subscribed to different market research figures, so thought they were correct and would issue press releases making contrary claims at the same time. Call them up for quotes, put the other company's figures to them and without fail you'd end up with a highly entertaining story about organisations taking chunks out of each other.

It was the same in the accounting software market. Sage, still the market leader, would issue a press release confirming this periodically, and its then rival Pegasus would jump up and say "no they're not!" - and we'd report it.

They were easy stories to write. The quotes were genuine. And once, I asked one of our readers what they thought.

Guess what, this stuff doesn't play well

The magazine on which I was working was aimed at technology dealers. They depended on IT to earn their livings, and predictably enough, they were left wondering why their suppliers spent so much time bickering in the press instead of marketing their products to make more opportunity for their sales partners.

Likewise, fun though Theresa's trousers are, Nicky Morgan's local Tory party is suggesting it has no idea what she's playing at. Whatever your politics, you can see that's unhelpful given that she's a Conservative MP.

We'll always publish this stuff. Punch-ups make brilliant copy and the readers find them entertaining. However, you don't work for us. The stakeholder readers, the ones at whom you're aiming, might well end up despising you for what you're doing. So avoid getting involved in verbal fisticuffs - and get some strategies under your belt to avoid being dragged into them.

What's an "exclusive"?

I had an offer of an exclusive story last week. It wasn't huge but nonetheless the idea that it was coming to my publication and my publication only was appealing. So when a press release with all the details went far and wide just as I was typing the story up, I was livid.

The PR company didn't seem to understand why. So here are some details.

I had a call from the PR people. They offered me a story exclusively and I said I'd be pleased to look at it. It was interesting and two days later they called back and I said yes, I'd like it as an exclusive. They agreed. So today I was in the middle of typing it and, as I say, I received the release - I checked with them that it hadn't gone elsewhere and I found that it had indeed, and that this was part of their normal conduct with an embargoed story.

So what's an exclusive?

A Facebook conversation I started seems to be quite divided about this. There are people who consider that the "exclusive" may have meant "nobody else sees this before it's released so you get extra time to write it" - which means the sites that just publish press releases get it at around the same time I did because they don't put the research in. Meanwhile I get about 30 seconds as the only person with this story on the Web.

There were people who considered that I should have published earlier - dead on the stroke of midnight - to ensure the exclusive (because all of my readers are poring over my stuff at midnight, of course). Many people thought the executive had confused the fact that there was an embargo with the notion of an exclusive.

Exclusive means exclusive

So here's the news, if you're in PR or organising your own publicity. Exclusive, to a journalist, means only one thing: you're not giving the story to anyone else. In the trade press and in the case of a huge story, this can be a silly thing to promise. Unless you have metrics to prove that appearing in a particular outlet will benefit you or your client more than any other, or if a major outlet will *only* cover the story if it's exclusive, why would you do it?

But don't, really don't, tell us something is exclusive and then send out the general release when we're typing up the story. Irritation and a general reluctance to deal with your company again will inevitably follow.

Know your terms

It reminded me of an occasion ten years or so ago when I was invited to a press briefing. "We're having a day of exclusive interviews," the PR person gushed. I asked, reasonably I thought, how you could have a whole day of exclusive interviews. "Oh, the interview Accountancy Age does will be exclusive to them, your interview will be exclusive to you..." she said.

Which might have been accurate but it was so general that it devalued the whole day, which would probably have done quite well if it hadn't been overhyped. Likewise today's "exclusive" - I would probably have gone for it anyway. I'll now be looking twice at any press release coming from that particular PR company.

"Exclusive" if it is no such thing is actually a damaging promise to make. Like "off the record", if your understanding of it is not the same as that of the person to whom you're talking, it can be a very bad thing. If you're going to offer an exclusive, be very sure that you and the journalist know just what that means.

And if you're sending it anywhere else, why do you think it's exclusive?

Five things a good media trainer won't do

Media training is something I enjoy doing. Helping people shape the message they want to get into the press, broadcast or online media and offering the tools to make this message heard is a great thing. Generally. Occasionally, though, I'm asked odd stuff.

Media training has its ethics

Sometimes the odd stuff I'm asked veers into the downright unethical or impossible. So here are five things a decent media trainer will never promise or offer:

- **We won't, or shouldn't, offer to write about you/your client immediately.** I once had a solid-sounding lead for media training. The PR person involved said at the last minute that they would expect me to write about the client in the national press afterwards. Guys, if I'm coaching you and accepting a fee, I can't pretend to the press that I'm an independent commentator. No ethical media trainer should write about you for several months after coaching you.

- **We won't encourage you to lie.** Want someone to come in and train you on withholding key information from stakeholders? You need to look elsewhere. A good media trainer will help offer techniques to get away from difficult conversations. He or she will give you the confidence to say when something is confidential and you can't comment. In no way should they encourage you to lie to the press - you're bound to be found out eventually.

- **We won't claim there is a 100% foolproof way to get your message into the press.** You present your case, you argue your point, we give you the tools and techniques to make the best of that. Unless you're doing paid-for advertorial, however, no competent media trainer will offer any guarantees beyond that in the face of a free press. They can do what they want with the resulting interview. We will equip you with the best chance possible to put a positive case.

- **We won't arrange interview opportunities for you.** This is the job of your PR company. I've been in training sessions in which people have asked me to get them into, say, the Financial Times. It's been a few years since I've written for that paper so even if I were inclined to step outside the role of "journalist/trainer", I wouldn't know where to pitch.

- **Related point: our contact book is our livelihood, not public property.** One or two -

a tiny amount - of clients seem to expect me to open up my contact book and hand over the names of all of the commissioning editors so that they can pitch to them. This is in most cases a step too far; if a trainer who is a current journalist had a reputation that suggested he or she would send loads of PR people pitching to an editor's door after every training session, he or she wouldn't be a journalist for long.

There's a great deal to be gained from a media training session: confidence, an understanding of the media, the ability to meet us half-way, formulation of messages and preparation for an interview plus a lot of interview techniques. Understand that it's a training/mentoring experience and you should end up with a great session.

Why do you need soundbites?

I've never liked the term "soundbite". They can look artificial and frankly calculated, and as a method it can be out of date. Think about Tony Blair and his "Education, education, education" or "Tough on crime, tough on the causes of crime". With hindsight, did that let someone into power without the substance and judgment he needed?

Let's not be party political. Remember "You turn if you want to: the lady's not for turning" from Margaret Thatcher. These are all getting pretty old, though. The popularity of Bernie Sanders in the US and indeed Jeremy Corbyn in the UK led me to suspect the age of the soundbite was coming to an end.

Enter Hillary's soundbite

I should have looked more closely at what was going on. "Jez we can" might not have come from Corbyn himself but it proved a very effective campaigning slogan indeed, and may do so again during the summer. However, the best example I've seen was yesterday's pronouncement by US presidential candidate Hillary Clinton.

She said, in one of her best speeches: "A man you can bait with a tweet is not a man we can trust with nuclear weapons". This is clearly a reference to Donald Trump, who has tried to accuse her of living in fantasy land.

The reasons this one's so brilliant, though, start with the ability to fact check it. The underlying assumptions are twofold. First, any US president has to be trusted with nuclear weapons (that's beyond dispute). Second, Donald Trump is a man you can bait with a Tweet.

So it's easy to substantiate, or at least to argue the point. Trump can't refute the suggestion by saying he's a lovely calming influence on social media.

It's also a soundbite that gives out a sense of balance, in that it juxtaposes one premise with another. On the one hand, there's the idea of nuclear weapons. On the other, there's the notion of allowing Twitter members to annoy or provoke.

This sort of tactic can actually make a soundbite work even when there's no link between the two. The fact that it sounds balanced gives it an air of authority (in this instance I suspect the link is genuine enough). It's satisfying and therefore it's memorable.

Oh, and did I mention that it's 78 characters long including spaces? That's handy for Twitter. Add a hashtag or attribution and it probably still fits. Nobody's going to tell me this is coincidence.

Do it yourself

Lessons from this sort of soundbite are many and can apply to any sort of business, not just politics. First, they still work, whether during an interview or during a presentation. Second, if you can embed some sort of verifiable fact in them and make them sound elegant, they'll be memorable. Third, keep them short enough for Twitter and other people will amplify the message for you.

This item obviously hasn't worn well in the light of Trump's victory – the point about soundbites remains valid, however, so I present the original piece here with only minor cuts

Broadcast interviews: what should you wear?

A while ago I watched a public speaking competition. All of the contestants were excellent but one speaker stood out, not because she was better than the rest but because unfortunately she was wearing clanky jewellery with a lapel microphone (also known as a lavalier). You could hear her clearly enough but the clunk, clunk, clunk of the necklace was just as distinct.

This can also be a problem in a broadcast interview. The camera operator or sound person will almost certainly want you to wear a lavalier, and it will pick up any noise nearby. So when preparing for a broadcast interview the first thing to watch for is anything noisy on your person.

A broadcast interview and a crisp white shirt?

When I media train in person I have a choice of shirts in which I look reasonably OK. The first is the old fallback, the crisp white shirt. The second is a selection of finely striped shirts - I kid myself they hide the middle-aged spread (if they don't, just don't tell me). Experience has told me, however, that neither is particularly good on video.

The stripes, though fine in person, can end up looking a little grey on a screen. The sparkly, distinct detail on the shirt ends up looking indistinct even in high definition; if someone's watching on their phone or other device it can actually look a bit grubby.

Brilliant white is better but not under studio lights. It can end up glaring at the camera, so the operator has to turn the lighting down or apply a filter - so *I* end up looking grey rather than the shirt! Off-white, pink, blue, are all good and will look fine in the studio.

Suit you, sir

The other thing to do is to wear something that fits and in which you're comfortable. Buying something particularly swish and wearing it for the first time, which is more of a problem for the female population than the "a suit always works" male contingent, can make people feel self-conscious.

For men like me (think "over 50") a decent suit is indispensable but be honest, does it really fit? It can be worth visiting a tailor. I have particularly square shoulders (tailors call this "squareback" which doesn't make me feel great) so off-the-peg suits always ruck up at the back. I started with A Suit That Fits and it's not as expensive as you might think (more than Marks and Sparks but less than a designer suit); many local tailoring establishments will be just as efficient at making something that works on your shape.

Finally, the newsreader Sir Trevor Macdonald always said it's a good idea to do your jacket up and sit on the tail, so it looks smooth. Bitter experience a little while ago says this works fine if you're reasonably slim and svelte; any signs of a belly and you'll look like a sack of potatoes. Without wishing to incriminate myself,

I've been doing my interviews with the jacket undone lately!

Please note that A Suit That Fits ceased trading in 2018 so anyone Googling for it will be disappointed. Anyone who's seen me in a suit will probably not have Googled for it anyway.

Get your message in early

When you're being interviewed on screen or on audio, how quickly should you introduce your prepared messages?

The answer is "flaming quickly". The reason isn't that you want to sound like a politician ignoring the question, that's always a bad thing. The reason is that attention spans tend to fall off a cliff immediately you start to speak. Statistics Britain suggests that you have just over eight seconds to hold people's attention. Four of those may be taken up as the interviewer introduces you.

This doesn't mean people will be switching off, just that they're likely to be less engaged after a short period of time. So what do you do?

Broadcast your message

The first thing to do, always, is to acknowledge the question. Nobody likes to hear someone ignoring the point completely. But you don't have to answer it immediately.

Consider this. You're asked a question that's nothing to do with your central message. You can answer it, or you could start with:

- That's an important point and I'll address it. First, it's important to understand...

- I'll get to that point but I need to make a few things clear...

- That's really important but before I answer, your viewers need to know where I'm coming from.

Obviously you need to remember to come back to the question otherwise you will sound arrogant. And remember a journalist will see through any flannel quite quickly so your messages will need to be thought through, unlike (to be non-partisan) pretty much either side of the Europe debate currently happening in the UK.

Answer the question but don't be afraid to get the message out there - your knowledge and authority is why they're talking to you in the first place, don't be afraid to use it!

Pitching: where are you going with this?

Pitching is difficult if you're in public relations. As a journalist I'm relatively busy I like to think. So when someone who doesn't know me calls up with a story pitch, it had better be good. "No thanks" is by far the easiest answer as I don't have to make any effort to produce it.

I was reminded of this today when I had a pitch from someone who'd been trying to get me to meet their client for ages. He would be in my subject area, they told me. He's interesting. You'd like him. Here's a list of dates, they said, so I gave in and chose one. Then they asked the deadly question.

"What questions will you be asking and what areas interest you?"

Pitching can be courteous but ineffectual

That just sounds polite but it was actually a difficult question. I was going because they'd been persistent, not because I particularly wanted to speak to the client. "Who the hell are you" is a likely first question, not that I'd phrase it as such, and other questions will depend on the response.

I threw it back and asked what their client would want to talk about. They ummed and aahed a bit. In other words, they'd spent ages and a lot of energy setting up a meeting for which they had no real objective.

Know your destination

This approach is often the fault of the client. Get me some coverage, they say, and the PR team finds itself measured by the amount of journalists' hands that get shaken. It's a faulty metric but if your client uses it, I'm not going to hurl insults when you adopt it.

However, it's better if you can work out some sort of game plan beforehand. Journalists are almost certain to ask why they should meet a particular executive, so tell us. We may well be receptive if there's a good answer. We certainly won't if there isn't.

Today wasn't the worst example of this that I've had. Many years ago (that's right, I'm off again) I was sent to a press trip to America. There was a party, and in the middle of it all the European press were yanked out because the CEO of a company called cc:mail wanted to meet us, we were told.

(Never, ever, drag a bunch of twentysomething journalists out of a party. Or anyone, if it's phrased like an order. It's just rude.)

So they dragged us out and put us in a room with this CEO. He smiled at us, we nodded frostily.

There followed 45 minutes of the most strained silence I have ever endured. I imagine he'd been pulled out of the same party and told *we* wanted to speak to *him*.

The PR person blamed the journalists of course, it was easiest - I do wonder how much longer she lasted.

If you want to pitch to a journalist, great. Don't let the fiercer ones put you off, we need interviews or we stop earning a living. Try, though, to have an idea of why we might be interested. You never know, we might even agree.

Are you paying someone to screw up your pitches?

I get a lot of story pitches in my work as a journalist as you'd expect, mostly from people with no media training behind them. And why should they - they're often start-ups, so I imagine they've just bought a cheap off-the-shelf template and are hoping for the best.

In fact I know that's what they've done. I know this because the similarities are too great to be coincidental. And the truth is that once you've seen one or two, they all start to look samey and boring. I start to switch off after a while. They don't work.

Where the template goes wrong

They run something like this.

They start with "I wanted to introduce you to my story" or thereabouts.

They move to some biographical information. Generally these people are into some sort of second career.

They introduce the second career and an example of why they think they're fun/quirky/whatever.

Then they move to "If you'd like to hear more of my story" or something like that, and conclude.

There's nothing wrong with any of this, particularly those that attach a picture. No, the problem is that they're so obviously using a template. There's no variety, there's no individuality - and importantly, there's no sign that the sender has done any more than a quick search and replace on something someone else has knocked up earlier and sold them.

Maybe it's in a book or maybe someone has started selling this as part of a "swipe file" - a set of Tweets, emails, Facebook entries and whatever that's supposed to make marketing easier. Only I'm telling you now, it won't work.

Talk to me, not just my job

You see, journalists are a picky bunch, for which you can read "egomaniacs". We make our living from getting our names into print - what, you thought we were doing this out of a sense of public duty?

So if you're going to approach us, you'd better have an idea of why you're approaching **us** in particular. If I were interested, for example, I'd probably turn around and ask why you thought I in particular would be interested. "Because you're a journalist" won't cut it, there are thousands of us. "Because you're a business journalist" ditto. "Because you've written about startups for the Sunday Telegraph" is closer but out of date by around a decade.

It actually gets back to very basic marketing indeed. Instead of saying "Hi Guy, here's all about me and my new business", try starting off with "Hi Guy, I've seen your stuff in the New Statesman and Guardian and thought I might be able to help with a piece for..." and carry on from there. It should sharpen up your message, it looks less scattergun and is going to hold my attention for a lot longer.

So please, bin the templates and for your own good, stop paying for them. Start from your desired end point: you want to get some coverage in the press. Then work backwards from there and arrive at your starting point, the right journalist. Target them, make it obvious that you've done your homework and you should get a fair hearing.

What sort of interview is this?

A lot of my media training is based on dummy interview sessions, and I'm often surprised that people just leap into the first exercise. They rarely ask for a scenario, for which publication I'm pretending to write, and what is the purpose of the interview.

Interviewers have to prepare for different sorts of event. If you know what they're after you're more likely to be able not only to help them but to use the opportunity to your advantage. I've also come across a handful of interviewers who don't consider the sort of piece they're trying to put together afterwards; these tips could help them, too.

Fact checking interview

OK, here's a completely fictional example: I hear a rumour that Facebook is going into the pizza delivery business. I've been bitten too many times by writing things off according to my instinct so I pick up the phone. My questions will be primarily factual, If my Facebook contact understands this, he or she will answer appropriately. On the other hand, they might assume I'm after something else.

A variant on this is the reactive news interview, in which I'd be asking Facebook what it had to offer the pizza customer. Trust me, they'd think of something.

Interview for a feature, looking for quotes

If I'm writing a feature on the pizza delivery industry and hear the Facebook rumour, the company might want to help by offering all sorts of quotes to pad the thing out.

This is great for me, maybe they say something like "Facebook has no immediate designs on the pizza delivery industry but we'd never say never. And we admire the people who ride those bikes and always deliver a hot product."

It's a deliberately extreme example but you'd be surprised how many people will try to say something vaguely relevant to help and end up with an on-the-record quote about something in which they really shouldn't have become involved.

From the interviewer's point of view I'll have asked more open-ended questions to elicit comments rather than facts. I'm likely to have put in more abstract questions to get opinions rather than hard truths and falsehoods.

The grilling

Perhaps I'm convinced there's a genuine story and that the underlying theme is that Facebook is losing money. It's hiding this and is desperate to deny it. So I go in harder - as a quoted company, Facebook is accountable to its potential shareholders. Remember the famous Jeremy Paxman and Michael Howard interview from years ago? Howard was home secretary at the time and therefore accountable to the electorate. As a trained lawyer he was determined to stick to his script. He's quite defensive because Paxman is being ruthless with his questioning. Paxman, meanwhile, can't think of another question (no, seriously, he admitted it on a Michael Parkinson show years later) so he more or less machine guns the thing home.

Sometimes I've found people take Howard's defensive view (appropriate in this case) when there's no need.

The profile interview

Sometimes you genuinely want just a chat with someone, some personality, a bit of background as well as the facts. In 2010 I went to Malaysia to promote my book, "This Is Social Media", and one of the journalists asked me about my favourite gig. There was no side to this, no agenda, she just wanted something more than "an author has written a book", which is hardly newsworthy.

I grant you, she then asked whether I'd actually seen the Beatles in the 1960s. I must have looked rough that day (I was five when they split up).

I've had interviewees behave as if they were expecting a grilling and acting defensively in the past when all I was asking was either fact checking or personality stuff.

A variant on this is the in-house interview, for a company magazine or website. I've done plenty of these on the understanding that I'm working for the interviewee's employer, client, publisher or whatever. The questioning will be softer and I'll often be mindful that as a corporate piece the interviewee is going to be allowed to check their quotes afterwards (and "I wish I hadn't said that" is an acceptable response). Occasionally I still find someone takes a defensive attitude.

Finding out what sort of interview you'll be involved in is not always a pushover but it can be worth asking. If you use a PR company it's easier for them to put the question; if I ask "will you be giving me a hard time" it sounds a little needy, whereas a PR person saying "where will this be going?" sounds routine.

A good PR agency will also be able to find out about the journalist and the publication, whether they have a habit of going in with the hard questions or are more likely to stick to the easy stuff.

Do try to find out what sort of interview you're doing. And if you're the interviewer, consider what sort of article, podcast or video you need at the end - taking the right approach will help.

Broadcast interviews: watch yourself

A Facebook friend who is a journalist had been to the launch of a new camera and queried the need for video as a standard feature. I commented that I always send people away from broadcast media training sessions with video of themselves and welcomed the inclusion of video on every camera; her response was that she hated watching herself on video.

Which is fine from her point of view as she's not one of my delegates. However, the media is going more and more "video" - YouTube is the second largest search engine according to some reports so you have no option, you have to take it seriously if you're building a business.

This means knowing what you look like on screen.

Broadcast tips

There are a few things you can do to make it all look a bit neater. First, ignore your instincts. You're going to spot that you don't look 25 any more, it's time to get back to the gym (I'm going today for the third time after a video interview last week!) and every stammer is going to be a stake through your heart. Nobody else cares about this stuff.

You can, however, put a little polish on. First, establish in your own mind which points are the most important for you to make and gently steer the conversation around to them (don't, though, ignore the questions completely). Second, make sure you're dressed comfortably - if you're buying a suit or dress for the occasion, wear it a couple of times before the interview so it doesn't make you self-conscious.

Don't worry excessively about your movements; I once trained someone whose PR executive stopped them every time they made the smallest gesture. They ended up looking like someone with some sort of condition, no matter how happy the PR person was.

Also remember to wear blocks of colour. Modern TV and video technology has eliminated a lot of the strobing that used to happen with older televisions but it can still look distracting.

Other than that, have something relevant to say and you should be fine.

What should you ask before a broadcast interview?

Broadcast interviews on television can be nerve racking. In the TV studio people will be able to see you as well as hear you, so how do you prepare? There are a couple of techniques I teach in my media training masterclass which ought to help. Here's how I learned a couple of them over ten years ago.

Years ago I did my first broadcast interview on a pre-recorded BBC show called Digital Planet. It was for the BBC World Service and my role was to comment on modern technological advances.

The first story was an interview with someone who was doing something in Zimbabwe. I was a little concerned as I had nothing to say on international affairs beyond what someone might have read in the papers. The presenter assured me there wouldn't be any difficult questions.

So he did the interview with the woman in question and asked me: "So, what implications does this have for the Zimbabwean position?"

Luckily it was pre-recorded so my first answer, a very long "Ummm......", was never broadcast. I learned two things on the spot and have stuck to them ever since.

First, the presenter might want to help but if he can't think of another question he or she might well ask something that will trip you up.

So, **second**, always ask what the first question is going to be. Most reasonable broadcasters will tell you so you can think about it in advance. As long as you've done your general preparation, you should get a reasonably strong start out of that.

Basic preparation for a TV interview

...is basically the same as prep for any other media interview. We'll take it as read that you know your stuff. Go in with three points you'd really like to make about the subject or about your business, get them out quickly and after that listen to the questions and answer them as far as possible. If you get a chance to talk to the presenter about what they need and the context of your interview, that's even better.

My most recent BBC interview, for the BBC London news bulletin, was better - so much so that they used my comment to trail the news item in the headlines at the top of the show rather than a comment from the company I was talking about.

TV interviews: where do you look?

Let's say you or your client have landed some television coverage. You're in the studio for the first time. I've been into the BBC news studios probably a hundred times. One of the first and most basic points I picked up was the answer to the question: where do I look?

There are in fact two answers to this. One is to look straight at the interviewer. Don't worry about the odd glance around, you don't want to go all rabbit-in-the-headlights, and if you're going to glance anywhere try not to make it at your watch, but mostly look at the person to whom you are talking rather than someone playing at being on television.

I can cite many reasons for this approach. First, you'll find it easier if you're talking to one person rather than imagining yourself talking to a few million. That's intimidating. Second, the interviewer will give you a focal point when all this other interesting stuff is happening around you. When I first did the BBC's newspaper review a few years ago I was fascinated that the television cameras moved around without an operator attached and had to focus very hard on not looking at them (I was also thrown by the fact that the studio was actually in the news room, although why I should have expected otherwise I don't know).

Third, you'll look more sincere. Remember all those years ago when Bob Geldof launched Band Aid? That's a reference for the teenagers, obviously. He kept looking at the camera and actually looked shifty and uncomfortable when he was delivering the most sincere and best motivated interview of his life. Look past the camera and at the person if at all possible.

Down the line

I said there were two possible answers. The other one is the "down the line" interview, when you're not in the same room as the interviewer. You'll have seen this on the news; Huw Edwards or whoever looks at a screen and a journalist or other expert/commentator appears to look straight at him. Of course they're not, they're looking at the camera.

That works and is a different sort of television interview - try never to get them mixed up and you should have a good start.

Radio: headphones or not?

A few years ago I made regular appearances on BBC Radio London. The best thing I did was to take in croissants for the breakfast show on my first appearance (if you do this and want a croissant, make sure you get one before the producers - eight pastries vanished in the 20 minutes during which I was on, not that I'm the type to bear a grudge). The worst thing was to put the headphones on immediately.

If you're ever in a radio studio I'd advise against this. There are a few reasons.

- Do you ever walk along the street wearing headphones? OK, let's suppose you do. You know how that tends to shut everything else out of your consciousness and things seem a little different? More particularly, do you recall how disconcerting it was first time around? That's what you want to avoid here. You'll be feeling pressurised; disconcerted as well is not desirable.

- Have you ever heard the sound of your own voice? If you're not used to it, having it delivered straight to your headphones as you speak can be really offputting. You put the "cans" on to look professional and now you're uncomfortable and when the presenter speaks to his/her producer you don't know what's going on.

You'll be a lot better off if you just try to talk to the presenter. Get your points in by all means, without being too forceful or impolite - but try to make it sound conversational and don't let the technology get in the way of a good interview.

Things not to say to editors

What should you never say to an editor if he or she is commissioning you?

I've been involved in setting up a new website for the New Statesman this month, editing numerous supplements for them and also editing Professional Outsourcing magazine for more than a couple of years. It strikes me that there are still some pretty fundamental mistakes being made by a minority in the PR and business world.

Let's make this clear: this is about people pitching commercially-driven articles rather than independent journalists or members of the public being interviewed. Journalists will know how we work and members of the public shouldn't have to.

So, some pretty fundamental errors I'm still hearing:

1. **That's the deadline? I'll try**. You're trying to be helpful, I understand that. But if you're going to struggle with a deadline, the longer I have to plan, the easier my job becomes. Editors get so close to the job (as do other professionals) that we assume you understand this - so when you say "I'll try" we hear "I'll definitely have the piece with you in plenty of time".

2. **The deadline is difficult for us this month; can we go into next month's issue?** The chances are this is a "no" because I'll already have the next slot filled. It gets worse. The person who asked me this recently was asking about a specific supplement for a specific magazine, so there would be no repeat of an appropriate slot in the immediate future; not only that but the magazine is quarterly. Anyone asking me about "next month's issue" goes straight into my mental "not a clue" file. (I do stress I'm talking to people who are pitching to me for their own company or client's gain - so I have the right to expect them to have done the basic research; readers and members of the public can make all the mistakes they want without prejudice).

3. **I've written over length, that's OK, isn't it?** Yes it is as long as you don't mind me making all the cuts I fancy. Editors, when they ask for 1000 words, mean precisely that. Technically you can indeed go over length on the Web, but if our house style is for shorter pieces we won't accommodate longer pieces. And on the printed page we don't have the flexibility. I've actually had people send 800 words for a 600 word slot and failing to understand that we can't fit it in.

4. **I've got a colleague/associate to write this.** This is probably fine as long as I know about it in advance. Next week there's a supplement

coming out from the New Statesman. I've edited it and there's a piece from an academic; it was prompted by an interview with one of his colleagues, who I initially approached. It was clear very quickly that choice 1 wasn't going to be able to fit it in, while choice 2 was probably a better expert anyway. They kept me fully abreast of this and re-confirmed when they'd made a firm decision; the resulting article is utterly superb. I've had other instances in which, at the last minute, having the layouts done including a headshot of the contributor, copy has come in by someone who's been a complete stranger to me.

5. **I decided the subject wasn't interesting enough so I've written about something else entirely**. Genuinely, I had this only the other week. Now look, guys, I'm the editor - and if I'm expecting an article on a given subject I don't want to be surprised at the last minute. Nor do I want to read an article that appears completely irrelevant after discussing it with you. If you find there isn't enough substance in the original idea I'm fine with that - pick up the phone, talk to me, it proves you're thinking about it and engaged! That's a great thing. Never, though, decide you're going to do something else and forget to tell me. For all you know I've commissioned someone else to write about something identical to, or too close to, your new idea, rendering it unusable.

The majority of people get it spectacularly right, most of the time. The guy in point 4 has written one of the best pieces I've ever commissioned, seriously. If you're one of the small number who do otherwise, please take note!

Don't let me ask myself this

When I'm writing something for the press there's a question I ask myself after every paragraph. That question is: "Why am I telling them this?"

If I can't answer that question then I abandon the paragraph and start again. Frankly if I can't see the point of a section of an article I can't expect the readers to do it for me. And yet so many people don't seem to worry; this is particularly true of some sections (by no means all) of the PR community.

If I'm reading your press release and wondering why you sent it to me, you've frankly lost me and I'm going to be hard to get back.

Reasons I may not be interested

There can be many reasons I won't be interested in a particular release and many are easy to eliminate. Here are some of the more frequent offenders:

- **The poorly-targeted release**: Just before Christmas I had a lavishly-illustrated press release on hand-designed-and-painted silk scarves for women. To the right journalist this had everything including images. To a business journalist writing about SMEs, Outsourcing and a number of related areas like me, it was of no interest whatsoever. The fact that someone has "journalist" in their job title doesn't mean you can send them just any old thing.

- **The poorly-written press release**: These are in the minority, fortunately. I still get the poorly-spelled and punctuated release from time to time and I try to rise above them. More seriously I receive releases in which the main point isn't clear from the headline, the thrust of the release is buried in the third or fourth paragraph or the point of sending it in the first place just isn't clear.

- **The release is of interest only to the stakeholders**: A good PR person is a consultant as well as someone who just does the bidding of the client. So if you're aiming to be a good consultant, please do tell your client that their new regional manager or their ten per cent uplift in sales is interesting mostly to the people working for them. Outside the business is anyone really going to care who heads up the sales team as long as they don't cause a problem?

- **The release with no point**: Sometimes I get sent a release that just tells me a client has an opinion on something. There is no effort to find out whether I might be writing about the topic in question, I'm just offered opinions. I suspect the client is standing over the hapless PR person insisting the release be sent; these releases fail the "why am I telling them this?" question immediately.

A lot of these issues are caused by clients who think that if they pay a PR person, coverage will follow immediately. They are compounded by the journalists moving about so much: yes, I get a lot of poorly targeted stuff but no, I wouldn't particularly want the job of keeping tabs on all of the thousands of freelancers like me in the industry. We get commissions in the short term that might well leave us appearing to be specialists in something we're not. That's the job, though, and the PR community can't afford to let itself off the hook because keeping track appears a bit difficult.

So before you send your next release out, ask why you're telling the journalist this stuff. If you can't answer, you might do well to redraft it a bit.

Things not to say to journalists

Earlier in this book I looked at things not to say to editors. Suppose you're an interviewee rather than a writer: what would be my top five things not to say?

In no particular order I'm going to finish this book recommend against saying the following;

1. **No comment**. Even if you genuinely have nothing to say, this sounds evasive and as if you're hiding something. I was once told "I don't want to comment and I don't want to read your paper saying I declined to comment." The thing is, the guy *had* declined to comment and it was my job to tell the truth. There's almost always something better to say; bridge into another subject if you possibly can. "My customers aren't raising that point with me, what they really care about is..." will get you out of a lot of trouble. I'm unlikely to argue with your customers.

2. **I'm not talking about that today**: Frustrating though it is, journalists aren't there to jump to your tune. Of course you want to focus on your own agenda but you wouldn't be this rude to a client - so try being a little smoother with someone who's going to communicate with thousands of clients. Your announcement schedule has everything to do with your

internal schedule and nothing to do with ours - try not to pass the problem on to us, we're probably not going to like it.

3. **Can we go off the record?** Loads of people use this one. If you absolutely must, go ahead, but be sure the journalist is trustworthy, organised enough to remember what was on the record and what wasn't and that you're both talking about the same thing. To me, "off the record" means unquotable; I've seen others who assume it means "print it but don't attribute it to me". If it could only have come from you, you could still end up in trouble.

4. **Your paper is rubbish**. Seriously, I've had this. You're entitled to your opinion and for all I know you have a point. But what useful objective is going to be served by annoying someone - not just journalists, in any context?

5. **I don't read the press**. You probably do a bit, since "online" counts, but that aside, this is a subset of "your paper is rubbish". Starting off an interview by trying to belittle the other person speaks loudly about your own insecurities, and most journalists are experienced enough to understand that. Try not to tell us you're terrified, we'll only scent blood...

Printed in Great Britain
by Amazon